The Hostage

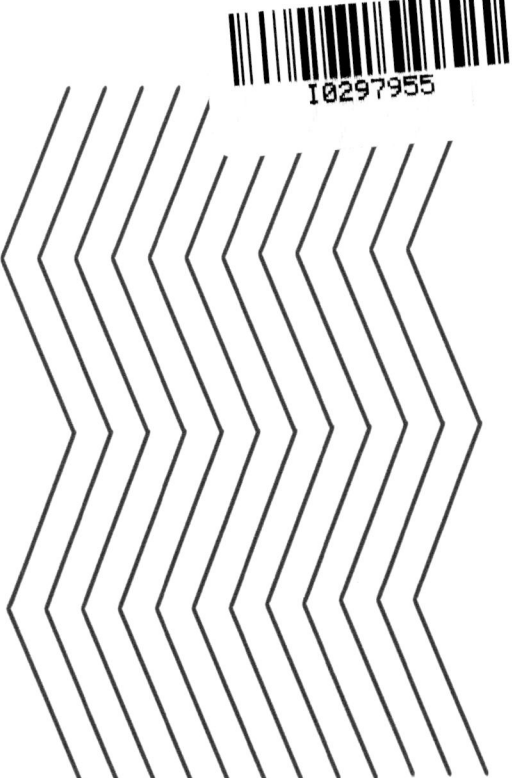

Šime Knežević

First published 2019
by Subbed In
www.subbed.in

© Šime Knežević 2019

Book design by Michael Sun
Cover design by Dan Hogan
Original template by Sam Wieck
Text set in 8pt Domaine Text

First edition

Printed and bound in Birraranga (Melbourne)

National Library of Australia Cataloguing-in-Publication:
Knežević, Šime
The Hostage / Šime Knežević.
ISBN: 978-0-6481475-7-2 (paperback)

Subbed In 008

All rights reserved.

This book is copyright. Apart from any fair dealing for the purposes of research, criticism, study, review or otherwise permitted under the Copyright Act, no part of this book may be reproduced by any process without permission. Inquiries should be addressed to Subbed In: hello@subbed.in

Subbed In and Šime Knežević acknowledge the Cadigal-Wangal people of the Eora Nation as the rightful owners of the land and waterways where this book was written and brought to life, and the Wurundjeri people of the Kulin nation where this book was printed and bound. Sovereignty was never ceded. Subbed In and Šime extend warmth and solidarity to all First Nations people. We pay respects to elders past and present. Always was, always will be Aboriginal land.

8	Easter
10	Home Alone
12	Palm Tree Neighbourhood
14	Countdown
16	On Beginnings
18	Cloudburst Moment
20	Hyper
22	The Harbour
24	Saw
26	time crisis 2
28	absence of the event
30	Logo
32	"Self-portrait" 2
34	"Self-portrait" 3
36	Seasick
38	North
40	Landscapes
46	After Yamasaki Kayoko
48	[That I might fill your absence]
50	After Celan
52	Fundamentals
54	Dearest,
56	Airflow
58	Variables
60	Edible Fantasy

Easter

They say
the scent of toast prods
the nose at our hour of death.
In heaven, I want to believe
every room smells like a
bakery—
I hope they serve more than just
hot cross buns, which is fine at Easter
but, forever?

Home Alone

The internet says the gunman is still at large
but I suspect he feels trapped, as I generally do, (also, I'm sure
the hostage too) *trapped* in my single storey red brick house.
The palm trees in the back garden, as framed by the kitchen
window, reassert bleakly you are not in paradise. I'm somewhat
embarrassed by this so I try not to draw attention to it.
I get regular approval from the gunman on how I want to
restrict view into the house, even if the sky outside is clear and blue.
I can see a blimp flying over my palm tree neighbourhood.
With the exception of the man that drives the lorry,
it's a really quiet street this one. The hostage rarely threatens
the silence too, so as far as I can tell this is a good hostage, I say
'you're a really good hostage.' The gunman hopes to exchange
him for a sizable book deal. I'm unconvinced of its feasibility.
The gunman will need a ghost-writer because of his limitations
with words, often generalising, or refusing to name. I've sensed his
    frustration.
Not far from here is a police station. I've yet to tell the gunman this.
I say out loud, 'I could go for a snack,' and I raid the cupboards.
Yesterday we ate all that was left of our main food supply. Only
what is edible is frozen. We'll have to do the shopping online.
The gunman gives a signal, waving in his personal language
I still don't fully understand, but mostly limited to a small array of subjects:
threat, panic, A-OK. When the gunman points I'm often uncertain with
exactly what the gunman is 'pointing to,' if you know what I mean.
I feed him and the hostage salted caramel ice cream.
Their spoons against the bowls are like the clicks of an empty gun.

Palm Tree Neighbourhood

We tried the next house. Dino knocked for both of us.
We stood parallel waiting for something to happen.
A person opened the beige wooden door.
"Good afternoon, sir, it's a lovely day," said Dino, "don't you think?"
I held the plastic bucket, heavy with detergent water,
with both hands, ready for Dino's cue.
"We're here, sir, to see if you need your car to be washed?
My brother and I are professional car
wash specialists and are always looking to earn some extra
cash. We will wash your car for ten dollars."
"Not interested," said the person at the door. "Before you
make a decision," said Dino, "let me say that
my brother next to me has devised a unique technique
in car washing and can extract water from a sponge
within five seconds and still have at least five minutes worth of
water to wash with. This is a new class of efficiency.
You've never seen this before. Tibe show the man."
That was my cue. I fished the sponge out of the bucket
and demonstrated my expert technique to the person at the door.
The person stood there nodding
even after I threw the sponge back in the bucket, and
he continued to nod when neither Dino nor me said anything further.
I saw a white cat inside the house step slowly into another room.

Countdown

The audience in their numbers look deep
into the livestream, stunned, by its likeness
to the shallows of a blue sea, a sky within
reach, likeness itself. The audience, in their
numbers, count themselves, grouped by
a shared countdown, to ascend and transform,
from here (the mess created by a previous
audience) to there (a deep blue sky), promising
this audience to replace themselves of
themselves, in numbers, empty themselves
of content, and float in the empty place
of images, ascend and re-form deep
into the livestream, become likeness itself.

On Beginnings

1.

I lose the regular rhythm
of my breathing whenever
I find myself in the airleaving
rooms of beginnings.

2.

I urge myself to hold
my breath this autumn
until next summer until
I make contact
with the warm hands
of beginnings.

3.

All my life I've found
myself before
the start of a life
that wanted to live longer
than the moment of
its beginnings.

Cloudburst Moment

They blame you, just name it, and
You take it personally like a love song dedication.
I warned you, time is want for pleasure,
People, so far, in their rumours, deny
Themselves the pleasure to swallow the hate
One feels for oneself.
It is like a fish-bone caught deep in the throat.
The truth is a rhyme and it rhymes with diamonds,
But *what* diamonds! Truth.

> They're reclining in their green swimsuits, in their
> Green chairs. In one minute they piece together
> The image of heavenly greenery
> To bank later on their white pillowslips.
> Denial is embedded in the airy machinery,
> How else do we access paradise, super-
> Leisure palaces for their own exotic sake?
> This is how it is, this is how it has been,
> Our ever-closing horizon, programming
> Claps with the Roland-808. Now playing
> "I would die 4 u…"

Now naked,
Naked now, releasing micro pools of funny ambergris
For the blooper reel,
A point and counter-point in 'the logic of feelings.'
I brush my fingers with my fingers,
I've always done this nervously before a confession: you're
Mind-blowing, on the verge of extinction. In uniform
You re-create daytime surveillance-scapes:
Lobbies, satellite footage of planet
Earth, puppies!

Hyper

^

Heaven's Gate, Heaven's Gate, Heaven's Gate, Heaven's Gate, Heaven's Gate, Heaven's Gate, ufo, ufo, ufo, ufo, ufo, space alien, space alien, space alien, space alien, space alien, space alien, extraterrestrial, extraterrestrial, extraterrestrial, extraterrestrial, extraterrestrial, extraterrestrial, millennium, millennium, millennium, millennium, millennium, millennium, millennium, misinformation, misinformation, misinformation, misinformation, misinformation, misinformation, misinformation, freedom, freedom, freedom, freedom, freedom, freedom, second coming, second coming, second coming, second coming, second coming, second coming, angels, angels, angels, angels, angels, angels, end times, end times, end times, end times, end times, end times, Jesus, Jesus, Jesus, Jesus, Jesus, Jesus, God, God, God, God, God, God

The Harbour

Our boat teeters toward
               the world. I eye by view of the keel
for the no-show dolphins we paid to watch en route to
the zoo. The harbour is showing off its shimmer.
       It's the summer of copious body glitter. We all agree,
       it's very glamorous, but
             Where are these dolphins?

Our boat encourages the saltwater to foam; it is otherwise
aloof like an out of office reply, or like the rings of Saturn, or
     a justification for war. Our city
is busy with itself, and fair enough, it has a hostage crisis
             to resolve. Things
in the scary waters of our innermost thoughts swim
       this way and that but, sadly, no dolphins
to ride finback victorious to the surface of this worry-dark sea.

       Suddenly, a sonic boom thunders
from no apparent direction. I
       see a trio of helicopters flock
             cityward, then a soft breeze presses
against my cheek.

Saw

after Handsaw by
Eduardo Berliner

I crawl away

The weight of your hour

Thrust on my back

You create a prison

At every turn

Who am I now in this—

time crisis 2

suddenly & momentarily
we form a relation emptied
of reference, if willing.

       the theme is vocal. thank you
       to the voice that says
       what I mean to say.

in the description field
we call upon the poet to
collect our

       lines, showcase us
       in biographical order. here
       we have you, a stand-in for me.

the time is over.
the time is over.
which one?

absence of the event

if passion eclipses
competency and

if outside the limit of
fantasy is more fantasy

(where you

materialise)

Logo

I am a simple gesture to repeat, a flow. I am a phrase
I never know when to say, for example, 'la grapefruit.'
I am a slideshow, I remember *thanks, have a nice day,*
and *that's a good song,* and *I really need some focus, honey!*
My bio insists infinite sleep is my best self and
my best horizon. In a world of shadows lapping,
nowhere to go and minimal technical support,
my dreams are, for some, on terror watchlists.
Death is a cartoon in my head. If I were near
an aquatic centre, I'd float on 'the surface of things.'
It's time to raise the stakes: I thought I was a knife.
I want to swim forward across the day like a shark.

*

"Self portrait" 1
"Self portrait" 2
"Self portrait" 3

"Self-portrait" 2

Of my towering brutalist body a residential thought plots to bray the sky in a thumb-war in a language I know. I ought to listen closely; careful, not too close. It should be clear how this process works. Thoughts like these tend to scare easily, run down the staircase, out the front door. And street-view: I'm 100% broken into segments, attached to this email, what a riot. I should keep quiet, tender my file system: Level_5/Room_4/Breakfast_table

"Self-portrait" 3

        I refer to the design of the body
        that glows with pins and needles.
        I refer to the body of the designer
        who identifies as a heat sensor.
        I refer to the weeklong humidity.
What happens to the person in this photo?
If you're blurred into ocean-like waves, I will cry.
And on hot days I will eat boysenberry gelato.
What else shall we do? Here is an old jpg of sweet
young pale me. "Take me home to your television."
        I meet me at the edge of the couch.
        My jaw adjusts by degree hourly.
        That you're not talking about it
        widens my concern. Hi, craterface.
Most of what I love I reject. It's me not you
operating on a working definition of 'maybe.'
I think as a loon, and it's a great way to relax.
I'm looking for literal boundaries not literary
boundaries. I love you as a poetic subject.
        Why the mouth? I cut myself
        into a quote. Consider this
        as part of an elaborate plan
        to transform myself back into
        a word. Consider this my origin.

Seasick

I make it look simple how I cross the threshold
of sea and land, but I get grumpy when people
mistake me for a meerkat. C'mon, have you
ever seen a meerkat make the sea quake with a jig?
I do hope we're on the same wavelength.
Because I live up to sixteen years, I am forever young.
They should make a movie about me, and I'll play me.
I have this little rumour going at the zoo that
I'm related to Hugh Jackman. (Get it? The Wolverine!
I'm not sure if you are familiar with my family network
but I'm related to wolverines. And weasels. And badgers.
Good times.) People often say they're put off
by my smell, comparing my odour to a can of tuna
left long in the sun, which sounds delicious if you ask me.
Over the years I've made so many cool friends online.
Tall poppy syndrome swims deep in my bloodline,
which is what happens when you were once worshipped.
Interesting fact, one of my Nordic ancestors was, quote,
the starting point for the Volsunga saga, unquote.
I do hope we're on the same page. Dear Script Doctor,
I have a serious crush on a mermaid, so my question is:
if I'm lovesick with a sea dweller does that make me seasick?

North

The hour is climbing a degree
perpendicular to
a cow chewing dark leaves.

Immigrants scale the void, their
purpose is obvious.
There is a train here too.

Kinetic energy relies on
the movement that preceded the movement.
I anticipate its revival.

In these final seconds
the wind
will experience light resistance.

In a way we're all lost,
or in loss itself.
Look up: flight and travel conditions.

Landscapes

1. Pond

The word "swim" brilliantly describes
an incertitude, a state of dislocation
latent in our flat world, on a steep decline,
a before and after, on the verge
of an ever near and at the same time
rupture of what is ordered, well placed.

2. Desert

When I watch myself walk into the terrain I see,

My experience of time becomes ungrammatical.

3. Cove

The tide breathes in and out
the foul stench of the rotten sea.
At least it has a sense of humour.

4. City

I think less and less about
the nerve endings on my feet,
yet in times like these I often
think on my feet. I'd be happy
to own a Rolex in times like these,
when I feel so misunderstood,
so unfashionable. Why must I be
perched as a sign that needs little
explanation? My limbs float,
coalesce, point to heaven and hell.
Somewhere in self-interpreted
discourse you will find me, vocalised,
a candidate for resonant frequency,
so that I might break glass,
bend bridges, as an utterance,
and dissolve, in the suddenness
of the next thought.

After Yamasaki Kayoko

little tear   and its tail
is swallowed   by the mouth
that tells   its story

its story   when told
has a backstory   a backstory
as long   as a waterfall

where   does the story go
when the face   dries
when   the drying hour arrives

tell me   tell me
what does the tale   of the little tear
say   about us

[That I might fill your absence]

That I might fill your absence, outline
Your body within the omission

That the space is blank, open,
Or is your blankness, openness—

You've receded in the chronological distance
It's characteristic of me to go back

I was influenced by you, your enunciation
Shaped my voice, there was gravity

I felt your body influence
        as it was wrapped stimulated
        around mine, pushing me in a sway

        I see this memory dimming, I see
        its trajectory, omega point

I am looking for you
        beneath the surface of this poem

I want you to emerge
        from the smoke, the hallway,
        the snow, the black and white,
        the cheering crowd, the silent
        grassland, the dining room

After Celan

It is the doubt that accompanies you when you leave the room,
the way you pronounce your consonants,
your rotating hand gesture to motivate a thought,
how in writing you address yourself in third person for attention.

It is also the weight you wanted to be lifted from you,
the dwelling I had lowered myself into,
the cigarettes I compose to keep you busy,

the night that follows night,
and the snore I hear in intervals.

Fundamentals

Above all else
Define reality: the limits
"Don't worry he only takes little bites"
    Also
Exoskeleton, a good idea, would it work for us?
For want of clarity
I place you in the x and y
And I drink water from a glass
        If you melt polystyrene in petrol it counts as napalm
I rehearse this moment
A million times
"Don't listen to the pillow," says a voice
    Meanwhile
In a field where houses melt
My final thought is, "What to do..."
The only solution is to stay with the problem
    So they say
It is either diagrammatic or representative
Of whiteness, commonly yours

Dearest,

I'm writing to receive a blessing
>	but I'm sceptical how this looks or feels.

In all the years of Catholic school
>	all I remember is how to procrastinate.
>	>	Procrastination is truly divine.

It would be an unusual time-slip
>	to collect my hands into prayer—

I wouldn't wear this look very well.
>	However, as evidence of my self-expression,
>	>	my soul is sick.

Shame clings to me like some dirty residue.
>	But I had always thought of the creative process

to act as some kind of wash cycle, a moral good—perhaps
>	the vibrancy of catharsis is spent,
>	>	sticky with sweat and empty.

Airflow

We have all taken our seats on the M5 ramp, westbound.
And from the ramp upward the sky clocks-off its blueness,
one by one another star burns through.
Our neediness beams doubly here, like two hands
locating whatever is immediate to touch.

My home lives in a mindless fuzz, too tired, too hungry
to be anything in particular. And it could be mid-week,
it could be the end of the week, but it feels like
we've been sat here forever and a week,
moving at a glacial drip into the tunnel with the heat on.

Variables

I ended up at the essence
of bummed.

I thought about addition
and eruptions.

There's a possibility
we're living on the precipice

as being
the dominant culture. Syria:

its trees, rocks, nature;
that proximity

to power.
The refugees are mathematically

reasonable.
In my equation most people checkout

in this world. A computer
replicated

some money and owned
art galleries.

I was like,
really? Let's go cat.

Edible Fantasy

In this ecosystem you push me into, I poke my tongue out,
to prove my worth, the ultimate taste test.
What fruit is in season now, it asks. Everywhere

I go, our civilization looks pickled, like Vladimir Lenin;
wealth taunts us like a gold tooth. Old money. When I chew,
I chew ethnographically. Bless you, comrade.

I rest underneath a blooming cherry tree (in description only) and
my tongue seems distant to me now. I think wealth
is lemony, and acrid, basically acidic.

Do I mean sour or bitter? Well, it all depends, right?
When I say bitter, do I mean nutty? When I say sour
—guess what fruit is in season now.

Best-case scenario: the seasons will blend
deliciously together like a mixed berry gelato.
Fingers-crossed. I should brush my teeth soon.

ACKNOWLEDGEMENTS

A special thanks to the editors of the following journals and anthologies, in which some these poems first appeared, sometimes in slightly different form: *Ambit, Australian Poetry Journal, Cordite Poetry Review, Lighthouse Journal, Magma, The Next Review, SAND, The Stockholm Review of Literature, ZARF Poetry, ZineWest, The Clambake: Cuplet 2018 Anthology* (ed. Claire Albrecht, Puncher & Wattmann), *100 Poets: London Spoken Word Anthology* (ed. Francis Byrne, GUG Press).

      The poem 'After Yamasaki Kayoko' was written for a Japanese poetry translation workshop at the University of Canberra's IPSI 2017 *Poetry on the Move* Festival. My sincere thanks to Rina Kikuchi, Jeffrey Angles, and Yamasaki Kayoko.

      'Hyper' is a found poem. The text is sourced from the meta-data of the Heaven's Gate website.

ABOUT THE AUTHOR

Šime Knežević is a writer and artist. His poems have appeared in literary journals, anthologies and zines in Australia, UK and Europe. He lives in Sydney.

ABOUT SUBBED IN

Subbed In is a not-for-profit DIY literary organisation and small press based in Sydney, Australia. Subbed In's program of publications and events aim to elevate the voices of trans people, people of colour, non-binary people, sex workers, women, people with a disability, LGBTQIA+ people, First Nations people, survivors, working class people, and anyone who finds themselves on the margins of the supremely white, cis, heteronormative, capitalist, colonial, ableist, patriarchal hellscape in which we live.

For more information visit: *www.subbed.in*

ALSO AVAILABLE FROM SUBBED IN

When I die slingshot my ashes onto the surface of the moon
by Jennifer Nguyen

HAUNT (THE KOOLIE)
by Jason Gray

If you're sexy and you know it slap your hams
by Eloise Grills

blur by the
by Cham Zhi Yi

wheeze
by Marcus Whale

Parenthetical Bodies
by Allison Gallagher

The Naming
by Aisyah Shah Idil

Girls and Buoyant
by Emily Crocker